Modern Nursery Rhymes

For Grown-Ups

Colin Moore

authorHOUSE®

AuthorHouse™
1663 Liberty Drive
Bloomington, IN 47403
www.authorhouse.com
Phone: 1-800-839-8640

Published by AuthorHouse   03/15/2012

ISBN: 978-1-4678-9029-8 (sc)
ISBN: 978-1-4678-9030-4 (e)

Other works by the author

"Top 50 Cream Tea Shops (that have homemade jam, bone china cups and a pot of hot water to top up the tea)" is out of print

"Plastic Bags—the Gold Standard in 2080" was adapted for television and renamed Celebrity Dancing on Thin Ice

"Westgate40" did not win The Booker Prize in 1998

For Pat and all puzzle lovers everywhere

With thanks to the following without whom this book would not have been written

Pat Moore, Mike Grimshaw, Karen Green, Karen Parsons, Brigitte McAfee, Michelle Bewley, Wikipedia and all those people who said it was a great idea.

About the Author

Colin Moore was born and raised in Bristol and now lives near High Wycombe. He grew up supporting Bristol City and moved on to Wycombe Wanderers. This goes a long way to explaining his sense of humour.

He was a Secondary School Deputy Headteacher for 20 years but led a double life as lead singer of Ted and the Boys. Musical differences-the band wanted him to sing in tune-led to his departure and a new career in writing beckoned.

Colin has always been interested in puzzles and games so it is no surprise that he has written these puzzles for people to unravel. However it is a puzzle to his wife that he has so many board games in the house.

Colin is still involved in writing music and is hoping that some of his songs will get into the charts.

Preface

It is generally agreed by most historians that this particular nursery rhyme, commonly sung in school playgrounds

'Ring a ring o' roses
A pocket full of posies
A-tishoo! Atishoo!
We all fall down'

describes the unpleasant red ring-shaped rash which was a feature of the bubonic plague. 'A-tishoo! A-tishoo! Mimics the violent sneezing which was a symptom of the disease and 'We all fall down' of course indicates death.

'Three Blind Mice
Three Blind Mice
See how they run
See how they run!
They all ran after the farmer's wife
Who cut off their tales with a carving knife
Did you ever see such a thing in your life?
As three blind mice'

seems to be about the execution of three Protestant bishops and noblemen at the request of Queen Mary 1.

Notice that I say 'it seems' because no one can be exactly sure of the meaning behind rhymes that were written 400 years or so ago.

So isn't it time we had some new nursery rhymes describing events and people of the modern era? Yes I hear you cry!

After all, since the start of youth culture in the late 1950s there has been an explosion of technologies and media which brings news as it happens into the palm of your hand or onto your living room television instantly.

So just as historians have made an educated guess, using historical documents, of the meanings behind our most loved nursery rhymes—it falls to you the reader, to try to work out the people or events behind the brand new rhymes I have written in this book.

Of course you do not need to trawl the archives of a library-remember them?-to fathom out who **'The black haired boy living in a bubble'** is? Or why **'Sammy Strongarm'** doesn't talk? You can try to search the internet or use Wikipedia!

I have tried to place clues so that the meanings behind the rhymes can be found. I believe that some of them should be easily solved but others may take longer.

More help and hints can be found at <ins>www.modernnurseryrhymes.com</ins> and if you would like to submit a solution to the 56 rhymes in the book, the entry form can be found on the website. The best solutions will win a cream tea with me-although if you are reading this in 400 years time you may have to locate my great great great great great grandson to collect your prize.

American readers will be sent a Bagel and a signed copy of the book.

If you have questions or comments or suggestions for volume 2 of Modern Nursery Rhymes then please contact me on <ins>cjm@modernnurseryrhymes.com</ins>

Lots of people have asked me which is my favourite rhyme in this book? I think the rhyme which has many clues and sums up the subject very well is **The Song and Dance Man**

The song and dance man
Burst on the scene
He was light on his feet
And his Tongue it was keen

He danced and he sang
Like no one before
He foretold the future
Then they fell to the floor

But his feet they got slower
His voice sounded thin
But he came back three times
He knew how to win

The song and dance man
Only shuffles today
His voice can't be heard
And his feet are like clay

The clues are all in this rhyme which depicts the rise and fall of one of the most famous people on the planet.

The rhymes cover politics, countries, music, sport, movies and much more. Not many major events escaped but I felt unable to write one for 9/11—maybe in time I will.

I hope you enjoy reading them and figuring them out as much as I enjoyed writing them.

See you for that cream tea!

Colin Moore
February 2012

Illustrations

All illustrations are by Mike 'MIK' Grimshaw

Mick is one of my oldest friends from Primary School days and aside from doing sketches throughout his life he is a prolific songwriter. We have written many songs together over the years.

Dick and Knave

Dick and Knave were fighting
Across the great divide
Fighting to the death
Until just one survived

But when the morning woke
They were still alive
Their armies had fallen
And many of them had died

But Knave he was not stupid
He understood the land
He offered Dick peace
But there was power in his hand

Dick and Knave were joined
With their forces they would rule
Knave was inside smiling
But Dick he was no fool

Dick would be the leader
With Knave right by his side
But would their forces be glad
To join them for the ride?

The Knave had played his Ace
Which betrayed his insecurity
But would Dick's winning hand
Lead to Knave's obscurity?

Billy Shears

No one cares about Mr Kite
Or where lovely Rita stays at night
They're fixing their holes to keep their sad lives in
Or getting better in the gym
And Lucy's the only one who ever hears
The sound in the night of Billy Shears

Where's the singer in the band?
He dressed in blue and waved his hand
He wanted help but no one seemed to hear him
We lent him our ears and he changed the key
We closed our eyes and he helped us see
He seemed so strange but no one seemed to fear him

The time it came for moving on
They didn't like each others songs
It was so plain but no one did believe it
The revolution never came
The wheels in spin the words in vain
He tried so hard but never could retrieve it

Billy dreamt of other things
On the run and spreading wings
His fame it grew but no one did acclaim him
His soul had died along Broadway
Nursery rhymes another day
Then at last the country did rename him

Billy wasn't in the band
But made the sounds throughout the land
They gave him thoughts he turned them into sayings
You looked on stage he wasn't there
Yet all his music filled the air
All you need is love was always playing

Billy Blonde changed the moon
The words meant more than the tune
Yet his tunes were always full of meaning
Sgt Pepper listened well
And overtaken by their spell
Soon Billy's songs were all that they were singing

No one cares about Mr Kite
Or where lovely Rita stays at night
They're fixing their holes to keep their sad lives in
Or getting better in the gym
And Lucy's the only one who ever hears
The sound in the night of Billy Shears

So where's the singer in the band?
Searching for the promised land
Just like so many more before him
In 30 years you'll understand
Why every single grain of sand
Has vanished yet the people still adore him

Spring into Summer

Spring into summer
The antelope said
Fall into winter
The ground squirrel said
The geese fly south
By word of mouth
Thanks to the seasons

Summer is warm
On the water voles back
Winter is cold
So the penguins go back
But what happened to spring?
Why didn't the birds sing?
There's no rhyme or reason

The world is not fair

The world's not like we've known
Said the king on his throne
As he looked at his riches within

The world is corrupt
Said the priest with his cup
As he forgave all of his sins

The world's lost its way
Says the preacher all day
As he counts all the money that's pure

The world is not fair
Said the leader with flair
As he takes all the tax from the poor

Waiting

He's been waiting at the platform
Waiting for that train
It's been a long time coming
But I see delays again

His mother seems so healthy
She's still on board the train
His son is even thinking that
The train can take the strain

You can almost hear him saying
'I hope that train comes soon'
For if it is much longer
He will have left the waiting room

Mr Angry and Mr Ice

Mr Angry always had his say
Mr Angry always got his way
His talent was indeed sublime
But did he have to scream each time?

Mr Ice never lost his cool
But Mr Ice he was no fool
There was no point to try to rile him
His frozen features were beguiling

So when Mr Angry met Mr Ice
On that Saturday so bright
It was a match so fine so tight
Mr Angry? No Mr Polite!

Simon the Cat

Simon the cat who got the cream
Simon the cat who lived the dream
Simon grinning from ear to ear
He was the one who everyone feared
The more he abused them
And didn't chose them
The more that everyone cheered

Simon the cat who licked his plate
Simon the cat who acted great
Simon climbing on trees so tall
Simon hoping he wouldn't fall
The taller he climbed
He just didn't mind
If people could see through it all

Flibbity Flobbity Flew

Flibbity Flobbity Flew
What is a boy to do?
I only asked for one
But ended up with two

Flibbity Flobbity Flee
It isn't only me
They say this and that but
What you get's not what you see

Flibbity Flobbity Flum
I don't mean to be dumb
But now those two have tasted power
They've become just one

Flibbity flobbity flew
They haven't got a clue
And when they have destroyed it all
We'll need more than just glue

He didn't Know it

Everyday
Things were getting closer
But he didn't know it
Words of love
Had come his way
But he didn't know it
Well alright
Learning the game
But he didn't know it
Early in the morning
It doesn't matter anymore
But he doesn't know it

Shining Brightly

Shining brightly
All around
Shining brightly
On the ground
Pure in love
She took his name
But soon she overtook
His fame
Shining brightly
all she touched
Shining brightly
Very much
Free at last
She took the hand
Of someone from
Another land
Shining brightly
So much in love
Shining brightly
Up above

Mr Bear

He had knowledge
That he wouldn't share
He didn't know
What they had there
he pretended
he knew what was there
He told us what
he wanted to hear
everyone knew
it just wasnt fair
But we sent them in
By land & air

But here is a man
Who believes in prayer.
Do we care
For Mr Bear?
For in his guilt
We all do share.
So do we care
For Mr Bear?

The Songbird

The black void went bright
When the songbird shone its beak
It's admirers we're amazed
And it's beauty they did seek

The songbird sang so sweetly
Its music filled the air
Soon it was all around us
The songbird had no care

Forthright it showed its soul
And it won many friends
But many birds were fearing
That it was near its end

How could such a voice
Be ruined and join the pack?
The songbird sang no more
It had gone back to black

The Black King

The White pawn strode
The White rook crowed
The red day dawned
The Bishop yawned
The black King called
The white knight crawled
The black White day
Was blown away
The White pawns struck
The black pawns ducked
The king was dead
The day was red

Stand up in the Bus

Stand up in the bus
Stand up in the bus
Did I hear you moan did I hear you cuss?

Bleak by name
Bleak by nature
Followed the law to the letter

Stand up in the bus
Stand up in the bus
Come on come on don't make a fuss

I'll call the police
I'll call the judge
If you won't shift if you won't budge

Stand up in the bus
Stand up in the bus
Everyone knows those seats are for us

I will not stand
I will not move
I'm tired of you telling me what to do
I'm sitting here
It is no sin
I'm tired of having to give in

The Black King Again

The black King
Moved his knight
And by day captured
all the pawns in sight

They followed him
Where ere he went
But some white pieces
Did dissent

They thought that
They could force a win
But the dream lived on
With the death of the King

Little Miss Baker

Little Miss Baker
Nothing would break her
She spotted her chance
She danced the romance
Then everyone started to make her

Little Miss Farmer
Built up her armour
And up on the screen
She was everyone's dream
And it seemed that no one could harm her

Little Miss Miller
Soon no one could thrill her
She started to ache
Then failed to wake
And no one knew of her killer

Black Haired Boy

Black haired boy
Living in a bubble
He came from church
And he caused trouble

He shot to fame
Coming out the rubble
Household name
Growing from a nubble

He passed away
Busy eating double
The black haired boy
Living in a bubble

Band of Brothers

The elder brother when in power
Always wanted to be king
All his followers said 'put your hand up'
But he never said a thing

Then his chance came in the contest
Now at last he could show his hand
After all the longing and the waiting
He could be king of all the land

But something strange was in the air
Isn't that just how it goes?
The union didn't seem quite right
And his brother won by a nose

The younger triumphed against all odds
And made sweet noises to the other
But as things settled they all knew
They had chosen the wrong brother

The Party

Who would like to hold the Party?
Asked the greasy Mr Smarty
We would—said the handsome Bill
We've done it before and got the skill
We agree said both the Daves
Everyone says that we are faves
We have the Party ready to start
'oh but you've missed the important part'
Laughed Mr Smarty 'very funny
You forgot to give me money'
'those nice people dressed in red
Will hold the party—enough said'

Little Boy Blue

Little boy blue
Played on his harp
His tunes were cutting
His lyrics sharp
No one was safe
From his fevered aim
Politicians judges
Were all the same
His fame it spread
The times had changed
The old order
Was rearranged

Little boy brown
Played in the mind
His images vivid
Giving sight to the blind
He distanced himself
From what went before
The people's shouts
Couldn't drown out his roar
With sweet Marie
He wanted to rock
He didn't care
Who he did shock

Little boy green
Played on his fiddle
On came the rhymes
And gone were the riddles
His voice was refreshed
His singing was clear
A new generation
Came to his ear
His lady laid down
She taught him to smile
But he couldn't rest
And was gone in a while

Little boy red
Played his desire
Back came the passion
Fierce was the fire
The wind was back
At the height of his powers
Reminding the fishermen
Holding the flowers
He conquered Japan
Once more being heard
The guard had changed
Just by hearing the word

Little boy White
Played a new tune
For he'd seen that the train
Was coming soon
He stood at the station
Spoke to the guard
Shook his hand tight
And played his new card
But times were lean
Under the red sky
The little boy's magic
Was starting to die

Little boy black
Played on and on
But the journey was empty
Yet the road was long
His voice it had groaned
To barely a whisper
But no one said stop
Not even his sister
So who will we remember
When time takes its cue
Little boy black
Or little boy blue?

Secrets

Well I know I like each all knowing secret
Initially it seemed cool
To tell everyone around
That our leaders are just fools

But is it everyone's tales
That you are spilling
Or just the ones that you think
Are the most thrilling?

Or is it just the stories
From the people who are free
Cos you can't get the stories
From the ones who are crazy?

So next time you are relaxing at the bar
And drinking
Just be careful what you say
And what you're thinking

Four Dumb Monkeys

Four dumb monkeys
Dancing on the stage
One poor monkey
Forgot to read the page
Now there's just three dumb
Monkeys trying to act their age

Three dumb monkeys
Skating on thin ice
One poor monkey
Slipped and paid the price
Now there's two dumb
Monkeys trying to win the prize

Two dumb monkeys
Trying to do the task
But one dumb monkey
He forgot to ask
Now there's one dumb
Monkey taking off his mask

One dumb monkey
Is the star for a day
But He'll be forgotten
Then he'll fade away
But for four dumb monkeys
They will always stay

Song and Dance Man

The song and dance man
Burst on the scene
He was light on his feet
And his Tongue it was keen

He danced and he sang
Like no one before
He foretold the future
Then they fell to the floor

But his feet they got slower
His voice sounded thin
But he came back three times
He knew how to win

The song and dance man
Only shuffles today
His voice can't be heard
And his feet are like clay

Tricky Dicky

Tricky Dicky sat on the gate
Tricky Dicky just couldn't wait
He wanted to get in
He wanted to win
He just couldn't leave it too late

Tricky Dicky forced opened the gate
Tricky Dicky thought it was safe
He searched in the dark
But set off a spark
Which lit up the whole of the State

Tricky Dicky said he was straight
Tricky Dicky gave them the tape
He blamed all his friends
Until in the end
He had to own up to his fate

Who can run further?

Who can run further?
Said Russ to Sam
Who can run faster?
As fast as you can

Russ started well
And was soon ahead
But then he stumbled
Sam thought he was dead

Oh no no
That's just a rumour you heard
But Sam couldn't see Russ
He had to take his word

Sam's training was bad
But race day was near
But with Russ out of the way
there was nothing to fear

Sam's trainer said
Everything will be alright
Just run out of the stadium
And then sit tight

And when the time came
He ran back in
It was all so quiet
Amid the din
He was taught at school
He had the right skin
The crowd went wild
Sam forced a grin
His secret was safe
Safe within
He had won—won the race
He had to win

Jack and Jill

Jack and Jill went for a drive
On a technicolor day
The streets were lined with people
All along the way

Jack would wave and Jill would wave
The were happy like at play
But just around the corner
Jack began to sway

Jill covered Jack, his head all red
Until the priests began to pray
The technicolor dream
Had turned to darkest grey

Let him have it

Let him have it
Go on hand it over
Sounds the normal thing you'd say
Let him have it
Shoot him dead
Doesn't get heard every day

But surely my lord
The latter's what he meant?
We need a scapegoat
And he seems heaven sent

Let him have it
Hang him high
We know wrong from right
Let him have it
And if we're wrong
We'll be out of sight

Stand up stand up

Stand up stand up
Said the father to his baby
You don't have to crawl along the floor
Stand up stand up
As his mother helped his first steps
Good boy now u can do some more

Stand up stand up
Said the father to his son
You don't have to take it lying down
Stand up stand up
Stand up to the bullies
You are the strong one they're the clowns

Stand up stand up
Said the voice inside his head
As the convoy in the square came inside
Stand up stand up
It was Man against machines
The world stood up and watched in pride

Kaa-ching

Dring dring kaa-ching kaa-ching
Dring dring kaa-ching kaa-ching
Are you there? Hurting hurting
I'm here to care kaa-ching kaa-ching

I'm in such pain Hurting hurting
Oh dear! again! kaa-ching kaa-ching
It's getting worse—hurting hurting
You'll need a nurse—kaa-ching kaa-ching

It's reached my spine—hurting hurting
Oh you'll be fine—kaa-ching kaa-ching
I had a crash—hurting hurting
Just bring your cash—kaa-ching kaa-ching

But I am broke—hurting hurting
Is that a joke?—kaa-ching kaa
I'm on my own—hurting hurting
Can u get a loan? Kaa-ching

I have no money—hurting hurting
That isn't funny—kaa

Are you there?—hurting hurting
Are you there?—hurting
Are you there?—hurt
Are you there?

The Sacred Symbol

The gleaming spires
The golden arch
People worship in their throng
Flaming fires
The millions march
To their shrine they can't be wrong

The sacred symbol
Like minaret call
Every age all through the day
The weak and nimble
The short and tall
Pay to speed their lives away

In every city
Across the globe
Temples have been built
They're not pretty
There's no robes
Made of finest silk

The non believers
They fight the tide
Of crimson with yellow stain
The worker beavers
To keep onside
As the followers come again

The sun shone on him

The sun shone on him
From the very start
But even at number one
He had a lonely heart
The sun got lower
It's power weak
As he lost Claudette
Down on the street
The sun went down
But his star shone bright
Solo and with others
He drove thru the night
Crying its over
Still the sun got higher
Only to die
In the flames of the fire
His sun had burned bright
But had turned to a gleam
As the sun went down
He was living in dreams

1000 friends

1000 friends
In your pocket
Hold them in your hand
But why they never come to see you
You'll never understand

1000 000 tracks
In your pocket
Hold them to your ear
You seem to be ever listening
But do you ever hear?

Joking Jonnie

Joking Jonnie
And his friends
Started out quite small
But very soon
They became the biggest of them all

Joking jonnie
He was always heard and always seen
No one was immune from this
Not mps or the queen

Joking jonnie
Left his friends
They thought it was a joke
But he stayed in bed
And he had a smoke

Joking jonnie
With his new friend
Finally got out of bed
But jonnie never joked again
Within hours he was dead

Bye Bye Baby

Bye bye baby
Why are you crying?
I know you're leaving
But looks like you're grieving

Bye bye baby
When you stopped the lathes
From working every day
I didn't see you wipe a tear away?

Bye bye baby
So when you gave the order
When the ship went down
I didn't see you cry I didn't see you frown

Bye bye baby
As you stood and watched
As the jobs all died
I didn't hear you'd sobbed I didn't hear you'd cried

So bye bye baby
As you say goodbye
It's a fine time
To wipe a tear from your eye

Fat Boy Westy

There lived a man called
Fat Boy Westy
Filled his plate
but didn't digesty
The same thing happened every day
He ate then threw the scraps away

Elsewhere in the town
Thin Boy Easty
Hadn't ever seen a feasty
He ate the scraps along the way
Then he struggled through the day

So what's the answer to this riddle?
Can't they just meet in the middle?

Little Nicky

Little Nicky had a tiny little trip
He thought no one would notice
But he made a little slip
David shouted 'you're in charge
So come home that's your lot'
Little Nicky hung his head
And pleaded 'I forgot'

Little Nicky made a major massive vow
But he thought no one would notice
If he changed his mind right now
A scholar shouted 'what's your game
You're just like all the rest?'
Little Nicky hung his head
And said 'it's for the best'

Little Nicky opened his tiny little mouth
But he thought no one would notice
If some rubbish blurted out
The dj shouted 'don't you know
You've cut warmth for the old?'
Little Nicky hung his head
And cried 'I've not been told'

Little Nicky had a tiny little plan
And he thought no one would notice
If the crown was in his hand
Someone shouted 'power corrupts
You know you've sold your soul'
Little Nicky hung his head
And wondered 'is that all?'

It's all history

Who will tell his story?
Who will know the truth?
He became so famous
Started in his youth

But as with every truth
There's no black or White
But within his story
The truth was out of sight

On the first of never
In his little world
Playing with the children
Little boys and girls?

But now his time is over
Who will tell his story?
How he lived and how he died
It's all history

Sammy Strongarm

Sammy Strongarm
Was the first
You really think he'd be so proud
Try to talk
Bout what he's done
But he doesn't talk so loud
You'd think the buzz
Would never leave him
That he'd want to tell his tale
But did something happen
On his journey
Was he the first or did he fail?

Obstinate Ozzy

Obstinate Ozzy
He was a wiz at sums
But was he?

Obstinate Ozzy
Said 'I can cut the debt
I'm pozzy'

Obstinate Ozzy
Doubled the debt then blamed
The snozzy

Obstinate Ozzy
If he lost a race he'd blame
His cozzy

Obstinate Ozzy
He was a wiz at sums
But was he?

Richie Rich

Richie Rich owned
all that he could see
And nothing could destroy
His tranquillity

But one day on his land
A commoner appeared
'how did you get this land?
Oh Richie tell me dear'

'my father handed it to me
The day before he died
Oh yes you were very lucky
To have him by your side

So tell me I'm intrigued
How did your father's father's father
Come to own this land?
There must have been a time
When it wasn't in their hand?

Oh yes in the middle ages
There was a battle held
My ancestor fought for it
Or so the stories telled

Oh thank you for that tale
But I'd like to own this land
So put your dukes up
And I'll fight you hand to hand

Greedy Gordon

Greedy Gordon
Had no pity
dipped his hand
into the kitty
he thought he was
like Walter Mitty
but left the oldies
in the shitty

Bright Bright

Bright bright
School had started
White White
The day was charted
Grey grey
Broken hearted
Black black
Forever parted

Acorn to apple?

From little seeds
big apples grow
mini apple cores
were fairly slow
but an apple in the hand
is worth two on the tree
when the pod burst open
two became three

just how a fruit
came to be king
its hard to understand
a very strange thing

acorn to apple?
it doesnt seem right
but its turned to color
from black and white

Too Much of Everything

There's too much of everything
It starts to wear you down
You want to see the master
But you end up with the clown
Everybodys listening
But they never hear
There too much of everything
And it starts to disappear

There's too much of everything
Senses in overdrive
You want to see the highlights
But you have to see it live
Media covering everything
Everything and more
Soon they'll be in your ear
And knocking on your door

There's too much of everything
Can't tell truth from lies
Wading through the wreckage
You forgot about the prize
Channels to the right
And channels so bereft
Nothing you can watch
Cos there's nothing left

There's too much of everything
And everything is bland
Research taking years
But now you got it in your hand
Noises in your ear
So silence wouldn't bring
Cos It might just get you thinking
There's too much of everything?

Sacks of Gold

Violence rages in the East
While tragic stories told
One Man working to make the peace
One Man filling his Sacks with Gold

Het and Pat

Het and Pat were playing their games
About the order of their names
'Het-Pat' sounds much better said Het
Pat said 'you're such a stupid get'

It's always been Pat-Het said Pat
Why can't we just keep it like that?
You'll do what you want when I'm dead
One of the truest words he'd said

Ic woke up disturbed by their words
And said 'you two this is absurd'
'Ic what do you think—tell us quick'
'all I can say is Pat-het-ic'

Free Schools

Free schools free schools
Anyone can come
Tho we'd prefer if you're White
Quite nice and not too dumb

Free schools free schools
Standards we will raise
We're not sure how we'll do it
But We're not just the latest craze

Free schools free schools
Why are they called free?
I know it is confusing
But it's as plain as plain can be

Public schools are private
But free schools won't charge a fee
We just take the money from the ones
Not like you and me

Ahead keep right

Turn around when possible
You ain't going nowhere
Better look in the mirror
To check that he's not here

Can't see where I'm going
Relying on my friend
He never fails to answer
When I'm going round the bend

He always makes decisions
When I'm at the crossroads
When I'm indecisive
He tells me where to go

While friends fail to text me
He never lets me down
If I end up in a cul-de-sac
He tells me to turn round

He'll never lose his temper
I can be in a mood
He's sweetness and light
And he's never never rude

I always rely on him
When in a busy town
my only fear is that one day
He's gonna run down

Staring at his blank face
Oh what would i do?
As I lay him in the wheelie bin
I loved him thru and thru

Should I turn left
Cos nothing's right
Or should I turn right
Cos there's nothing left?

Cut cut cut

Cut cut cut
They kept cutting
Once they started
There was no stopping

Teachers nurses doctors too
Hurry up there's lots to do
Don't forget the boys in blue
Army navy and public loos

Cut the grant to the arts
They're not really worth their parts
Libraries museums—all the farts
But please don't touch the queen of hearts

The question no one seems to ask
Is when they've finished this vicious task
When we look behind their mask
Up to the open furnace cast

Will there be anything left?

The circle

The circle comes around
Every four years or so
The cheering of the crowds
The speeches we all know

The circle carries round
With trouble toil and strife
As if a new beginning
Will make a change to life

Why can't we learn from history?
Nothings perfect as it sounds
Sometimes it's 'no we can't
As the circle turns around

Mary Mary Quite Contrary

Mary Mary
Quite contrary
The guardian of our soul
Making sure that nothing
Could corrupt us being whole

Mary Mary
Never vary
Standing up so tall
Not mistaking progress
For the freshness of it all

Mary Mary
Quite contrary
We smiled at every row
But see the mess since you've gone
And We're not laughing now

Famey Famey

Famey Famey
Oh so samey
Sing your same old song
Famey Famey
I don't blamey
If it bangs a gong

Swishy Swishy
Looking dishy
On the sea of red
Swishy Swishy
Need a tishy
As u hold your head

Clappy Clappy
Let's look happy
As u stand and cheer
Clappy Clappy
Where's the pappy?
Hey I'm over here

Famey Famey
Play the gamey
From your ivory view
Famey Famey
What's your namey?
When your time is through

Twinkletoes

Twinkletoes
Magic feet
Call him what you will
Even those against him
Marvelled at his skill

Underhand
Overhead
Call him what you will
People turned against him
They had had their fill

Crazy eyes
Purple lies
Call him what you will
No longer magic feet
Bring on magic pill

Twinkletoes
Magic feet
Underhand
Overhead
Crazy eyes
Purple lies
Call him what you will

Robert and Bo

Robert had a challenge
To beat Bo the Red
His country was behind him
But it was pounding through his head

Did they really want him
Or was it just national pride?
should he take the challenge up?
It was eating him inside

He nearly missed an opening
He struggled at the start
But Bo felt the pressure
And Robert he took heart

The drawn out game was over
Well before the end
Robert had triumphed
His nation had a friend

History it beckoned
But Robert hid away
Through the dark and dirty streets
He never saw the day

People talk of what could have been
But His story is so sad
The greatest of them all?
Genius or mad?

Grand Old Duke Of Naught

The grand old duke he toured the world
Thru all the countries north and south
He tried to put his best foot forward
But it ended up inside his mouth

The grand old duke he had no men
But many thought him shrewd
If there was something he didn't like
He just ended up being rude

The grand old duke he didn't care
Perhaps he'd been badly taught
But on his epitaph plain to see
The grand old duke of naught

Wonderland

Dusting down through your 45s
Where the infinite jukebox never dies
As the jump on the track
Brings the memory back
And the name on the cover
Was your very first lover

Jimmy on Luxemburg played the start
Then The Pirates played their part
The jukebox played it through
But it always seemed brand new
And the name on the cover
Was your very first lover

Clutching the disc in your hand
Til you got home to your wonderland
The crackles and the hiss
You just didn't care
And as the needle dropped
Wonderland . . . was there

Through the tears of a clown
And the tracks of your tears
Songs were your life thru All Of the years
Behind a painted smile
You lived all the while
And the name on the cover
Was your very first lover

But reality went away
When you got home to play
The voices outside
You just didn't hear
And as the needle began to fall
Wonderland . . . was near

The vinyl left and 8 track too
The music lived on and on In you
you discovered Jon
Kurt turned you on
And the name on the cover
Was your very first lover

Downloading all your tracks
Your memories come flooding back
Of when you were young
And oh how time flies
Although the needle's gone
Wonderland . . . Never dies

Bibliography

Wikipedia-a very under-rated resource

Hey Diddle Diddle by Sam Foster published by Summersdale